TRIBES of NATIVE AMERICA

Comanche

edited by Marla Felkins Ryan
and Linda Schmittroth

**BLACKBIRCH®
PRESS**

THOMSON

GALE

San Diego • Detroit • New York • San Francisco • Cleveland
New Haven, Conn. • Waterville, Maine • London • Munich

THOMSON

GALE

LIBRARY OF CONGRESS CATALOGING-IN-PUBLICATION DATA

Comanche / Marla Felkins Ryan, book editor ; Linda Schmittroth, book editor.
    v. cm. — (Tribes of Native America)
Includes bibliographical references.
Contents: Comanche name — Origins and group affiliations — Buffalo war — Religion — Government — Daily life — Customs — Current tribal issues.
  ISBN 1-56711-689-2 (alk. paper)
  1. Comanche Indians—Juvenile literature. [1. Comanche Indians. 2. Indians of North America—Great Plains. 3. Indians of North America—Southwest, New.] I. Ryan, Marla Felkins. II. Schmittroth, Linda. III. Series.

E99.C85 C47 2003
978.004'9745—dc21   2002015823

Printed in United States
10 9 8 7 6 5 4 3 2 1

Table of Contents

COMANCHE

Name

The Comanche (pronounced *cuh-MAN-chee*) called themselves Nerm, which means "people." Comanche probably came from the Ute word for the tribe, Koh-Mahts. It means "anyone who wants to fight me all the time."

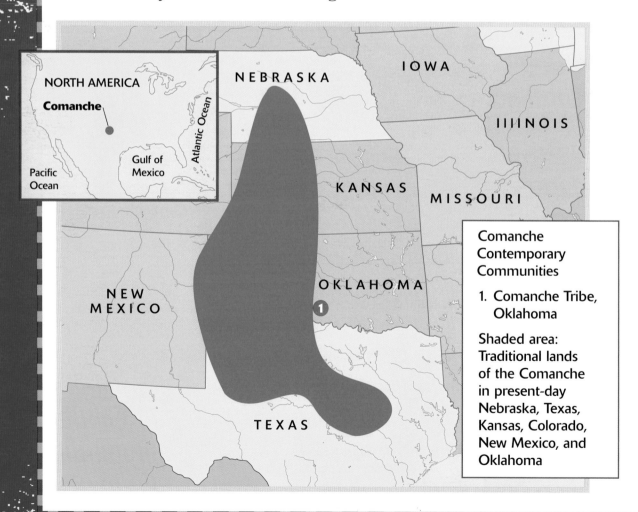

NORTH AMERICA

Comanche

Pacific Ocean

Gulf of Mexico

Atlantic Ocean

NEBRASKA

IOWA

IIIINOIS

KANSAS

MISSOURI

NEW MEXICO

OKLAHOMA

①

TEXAS

Comanche Contemporary Communities

1. Comanche Tribe, Oklahoma

Shaded area: Traditional lands of the Comanche in present-day Nebraska, Texas, Kansas, Colorado, New Mexico, and Oklahoma

The Comanche used horses to travel across their homeland in the Southwest.

Where are the traditional Comanche lands?

The Comanche roamed the southern Great Plains. Parts of their lands make up a large section of the Southwest, including present-day Texas, Colorado, and New Mexico. Today, descendents of the Comanche share a reservation with the Kiowa and Apache. It is 87 miles southwest of Oklahoma City, Oklahoma.

What has happened to the population?

There were about 20,000 Comanche in the early 1800s. The population went down to 1,500 in 1900 because of wars and diseases. In a 1990 count of the population by the U.S. Census Bureau, 11,267 people said they were Comanche.

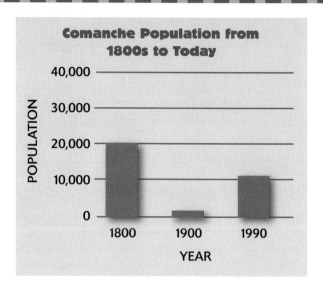

Comanche Population from 1800s to Today

POPULATION

40,000
30,000
20,000
10,000
0

1800   1900   1990

YEAR

Origins and group ties

The Comanche were part of the Shoshone tribe until the 1600s. The Comanche then split from the Shoshone and moved south from Wyoming and Montana.

This painting by famed artist George Catlin shows Comanche war parties. The Comanche fought Spanish and American armies across the southern Great Plains.

Often called the Lords of the Southern Plains, the Comanche once controlled a vast land. The Spanish called the region Comanchería, or "land of the Comanche." The Comanche were a loosely organized group of horsemen and warriors who wandered from place to place. At one time or another, they fought nearly every other Plains tribe. They also took on the Spanish and American armed forces to defend their lands.

This illustration shows a battle between the Comanche and the Ute.

HISTORY

Horses change lifestyle

The Comanche broke off from their relatives, the Shoshone, in the late 1600s. They moved south from Wyoming and Montana to the Great Plains. Sometime before 1705, they got horses from the Ute. The Ute had been given the animals by the Spanish in Mexico. The lives of the Comanche, who had always wandered on foot, changed a great deal. By 1750, the Comanche had become

The Comanche were skilled horse riders.

skilled riders. Over the next 100 years, the tribe came to own more horses than any other tribe.

Sometimes the tribe carried out raids on other Indians or on white settlers to get horses. The Comanche, though, also knew how to breed and train horses, unlike most other tribes.

Horses helped the Comanche control a huge amount of land. Between 1750 and 1875, the Comanche spread across Kansas and Texas, and through the rest of the Southwest. This 24,000-square-mile area was called the Comanchería.

Trade, raids, and war

The Comanchería was between lands claimed by Spain in the Southwest and by France in Louisiana. The Comanche traded with both the Spanish and the French. The Comanche traded prisoners of war to be used as slaves by the Spanish. They traded buffalo hides with the French. In return, they got horses from the Spanish and guns from the French.

In the early 1800s, outside events had big effects on the Comanche. In the Louisiana Purchase of 1803, France sold a huge tract of land to the United States. The land reached from the Mississippi River in the east to the Rocky Mountains in the west. It ran from the Gulf of Mexico in the south to Canada in the north.

1869
The Transcontinental Railroad is completed

1874-1875
The Comanche make their last stand; Quanah Parker and his followers surrender and go to a reservation

1914–1918
WWI is fought in Europe

1929
Stock market crash begins the Great Depression

1941
Bombing at Pearl Harbor forces United States into WWII

1945
WWII ends

1950s
Reservations no longer controlled by federal government

1967
The Comanche adopt a tribal constitution

Comanche warriors battled white settlers to protect their land.

Now that it owned this vast new area, the U.S. government wanted to give Americans more land. To do this, the government forced eastern Indian tribes to move west of the Mississippi River. There, the tribes competed with the Comanche on the Great Plains for a share of the buffalo herds. Soon, American settlers pressed close to the borders of the Comanchería. The situation got even worse for the Comanche after Mexico won control of Texas from Spain in 1821. Mexican settlers began to move in and take over more Comanche lands.

The Comanche fought the newcomers fiercely. Sometimes they killed white hunters and traders and took captives.

Problems in Texas

In 1845, the Texas Revolution freed Texas from Mexican rule. American settlers moved to ranches and farms there. They made easy targets for Comanche raids. The Texas Rangers (a police group) often fought with the Comanche. In 1838, Texas Rangers tried to capture Comanche leaders who had come to take part in peaceful negotiations. Thirty-five Comanche were killed, and many others were wounded. Over the next three decades, Texas became part of the United States, and gold was found in California.

This engraving shows a Texas Ranger. The Texas Rangers fought many battles with the Comanche.

More settlers poured into Texas, and goldminers galloped across the Comanchería. As they moved, they spread diseases and threw off the movements of the buffalo herds. Made weak by disease and hunger, the Comanche still fought on. They had a short period of relief during the American Civil War (1861–1865). After that, though, the U.S. government set out to end the violence on the Great Plains once and for all.

The Comanche and other Native Americans fought white buffalo hunters.

The Buffalo War

After the Civil War, the Comanche had to deal with both the Texas Rangers and the full force of the U.S.

military. Then, in the 1870s, whites began to kill off what was left of the buffalo herds.

In 1874, a band of Comanche led by Chief Quanah Parker (lived from about 1852 to 1911) tried to stop this slaughter. The Comanche attacked a group of buffalo hunters. This event marked the start of the Red River War (also known as the Buffalo War). After U.S. troops killed hundreds of horses and burned the tribe's food and tepees, most of the Comanche surrendered.

Quanah Parker and his followers held out until June 1875. When Parker and his people went to a reservation in Oklahoma, nearly 200 years of Comanche power came to an end.

Chief Quanah Parker led an attack against buffalo hunters in 1874.

On the reservation

The U.S. government tried to make the Comanche become farmers. It also tried to force them to accept American ways. The Comanche had to depend on the Bureau of Indian Affairs for basic needs such as food and clothing. Since then, the Comanche have faced hunger and poverty, and have continued to lose their land. Still, the Comanche proudly fight to hold on to their traditions.

Some Comanche believed that wolves were their ancestors.

Religion

The Comanche did not believe in a creator god. They thought they had come from animals, perhaps wolves. They believed supernatural powers lived in rocks and animals. If the people pleased these powers, they could get the favors they needed to survive.

Religion was seen as a private matter. There were no special religious leaders. The Comanche thought the spirits of the dead lived forever in a land where there was plenty of game and fast horses. Almost everyone who died had an afterlife. Only warriors who were scalped in battle did not live after death.

Unhappy with reservation life, some Comanche found comfort in the Peyote (pronounced *pay-OH-tee*) Religion. As part of this faith, the people took peyote. This drug comes from cactus and may give the user visions. In 1918, the Peyote Religion led to the founding of the Native American Church. This faith used both native and Christian practices.

This Comanche man was a leader in the Peyote Religion.

Government

Comanche groups had no real leaders except those who were chosen to lead during wars. After a war ended, the war leaders lost their power. Before decisions were made, all those who wished to speak were allowed to have their say. All adult males in the group had to agree with the decision. If a man could not agree with the rest of the group, he left and joined another group. Women had no say in the group's decisions.

Wallace Coffey is a former Comanche tribal chairman.

Comanche Charles Chibitty received an award for serving in the U.S. Army during World War II.

The Comanche adopted a tribal constitution in 1967. Today, the tribe is run by a tribal council. The council elects a business committee with seven members. Members serve three-year terms.

Economy

The Comanche economy changed in the 18th century. Before then, the people gathered and hunted on foot. After 1700, the economy grew. Horses and slaves were traded to the Spanish for more horses. The Comanche also traded with the French for guns and luxury items.

After the move to the reservation, the Comanche tried to farm, but most of the land was not good for farms. They also raised cattle and worked for white farmers and ranchers. Today, they still do these jobs. They also lease out mineral rights and rights to raise cattle on their lands. There are small businesses on the reservation, too. Among these are a bingo hall and a smoke shop.

Some Comanche have served in the American armed forces. Many also work off the reservation in oil fields or in skilled occupations.

DAILY LIFE

Families

Families were made up of parents, children, and other close relatives. Because life was hard and many children died young, all children were treasured.

Adults always worked hard. Men hunted and fought wars. When they were too old for this, they made bows and arrows. Women did all the other jobs.

Comanche women dried meat for food and hides for clothing.

Education

Grandparents played a large role in child rearing. To learn about life, children watched and imitated adults. They learned at a young age their main task: to make sure there was enough food.

On the reservation, Christian missionaries and the government set up schools. They hoped to make Comanche children give up their native culture. Comanche parents did not want this, so few children went to the schools. Comanche children who go to Oklahoma public schools today still have problems. This is often because of cultural differences.

Like many other Native American tribes who lived on the Great Plains, the Comanche lived in tepees.

Buildings

The Comanche moved with the buffalo or when they needed new grass to feed their horses. They had to have homes that could be put up and taken down quickly. Their tepees were made of four base poles stuck into the ground. The poles were tied together at the top to form a cone shape. Buffalo hides were stretched around the frame. In the summer, the hide covers were rolled up to let in fresh air.

Food

Buffalo was the main food, but the Comanche also hunted elk, bear, and other game. When game was scarce, they ate horses. They did not eat dogs, which they saw as relatives of their ancestors, the wolves. They did not eat fish, either. They would also not eat fowl unless they faced starvation. They thought it was food for cowards. When white ranchers began to raise cattle nearby, the tribe often raided the herds and got beef to eat.

The Comanche did not farm, but they got plant foods in other ways. They traded with other tribes for corn, and gathered wild plants, such as grapes and plums. A favorite food was pemmican. This cake-like dish was made of dried buffalo meat and different nuts and berries.

The Comanche's main food was buffalo meat. They also used buffalo hides to make clothing and tepees.

Men's clothing

Everyday clothing was plain and practical. Clothing worn to make war, though, was colorful and elegant. Comanche men usually wore a buckskin breechcloth (a piece of material that wrapped between the legs and tucked into a belt). Fringed buckskin leggings that reached from the belt to the ankles were also worn. So were buckskin moccasins with tough, buffalo-hide soles. Men rarely wore shirts.

Comanche men wore colorful breechcloths and leggings in times of war.

Most often, young boys went naked until they were nine or ten, when they began to wear adult clothes.

Comanche men had long hair that they parted in the middle. They often painted their scalps where the hair was parted. They wore braids on each side of their faces. A tiny braid known as a scalplock hung over the forehead. It was often decorated with cloth, beads, and a feather. Comanche men plucked their face and body hair, even their eyebrows.

In winter, the Comanche wore knee-high boots and buffalo robes for warmth.

Women's clothing

Comanche women wore moccasins with one-piece buckskin dresses that had flared skirts and fringe. Unlike boys, girls always wore clothing. Women's special-occasion clothes had beads and bits of metal that made sounds. Women cut their hair short and painted their faces and bodies in bright colors. In the winter, all Comanche tribe members wore heavy buffalo robes and knee-high boots for warmth.

George Woogee Watchetaker was a Comanche medicine man.

Healing practices

The Comanche had hard lives and often faced great suffering. People learned early to handle severe pain. Doctors were hunter-warriors who had special skills. They knew how to do minor surgery. They used herbs to treat wounds and cure illnesses. They even knew how to fill cavities in teeth. Sometimes, older women served as doctors.

Arts

The Comanche always had to search for food. They had little time for art. There were few songs and dances or ceremonies. Men did take special care when they made and decorated their war shields, though.

CUSTOMS

War and hunting rituals

Before a hunt, the Comanche prayed to the buffalo spirit for a good catch. To hunt, they surrounded a group of buffalo with their horses. Then they killed as many animals as they could with lances or bows and arrows. Sometimes they made a herd of buffalo run off the edge of a cliff. When a man hunted alone, he wore buffalo robes as a disguise so he could sneak up on the herd.

Comanche war parties often traveled long distances to fight.

WHY THE BEAR WADDLES WHEN HE WALKS: A COMANCHE TALE

In the beginning days, nobody knew what to do with the Sun. It would come up and shine for a long time. Then it would go away for a long time, and everything would be dark.

The daytime animals naturally wanted the Sun to shine all the time, so they could live their lives without being interrupted by the dark. The nighttime animals wanted the Sun to go away forever, so they could live the way they wanted to.

At last they all got together, to talk things over.

Old Man Coyote said, "Let's see what we can do about that Sun. One of us ought to have it, or the other side ought to get rid of it."

"How will we do that?" Scissor-tailed Flycatcher asked. "Nobody can tell the Sun what to do. He's more powerful than anyone else in the world."

"Why don't we play hand game for it?" Bear asked. "The winning side can keep the Sun or throw it away, depending on who wins and what they want to do with it."

So they got out the guessing bones to hide in their hands, and they got out the crow-feathered wands for the guessers to point with, and

According to Comanche legend, the bear was a night animal that wanted the sun to go away forever.

they got out the twenty pointed dogwood sticks for the umpires to keep score with. Coyote was the umpire for the day side, and nighttime umpire was Owl. The umpires got a flat rock, like a table, and laid out their counting sticks on that. Then the two teams brought logs and lined them up facing one another, with the umpires and their flat rock at one end between the two teams.

That was a long hand game. The day side held the bones first, and they were so quick and skillful passing them from hand to hand behind their backs and waving them in the guessers' faces that it seemed surely they must win. Then Mole, who was guessing for the night side, caught both Scissor-tail and Hawk at the same time, and the bones went to the night side, and the day people began to guess.

Time and again the luck went back and forth, each team seeming to be about to beat the other. Time and again the luck changed, and the winning team became the losing one.

The game went on and on. Finally the Sun, waiting on the other side of the world to find out what was going to happen to him, got tired of it all.

The game was so long that Bear got tired, too. He was playing on the night side. He got cramped sitting on the log, and his legs began to ache. Bear took off his moccasins to rest his feet, and still the game went on and on.

At last the Sun was so bored that he decided to go and see for himself what was happening. He yawned and stretched and crawled out of his bed on the underneath side of the world. He started to climb up his notched log ladder to the top side, to find out what was happening.

As the Sun climbed, the light grew stronger, and the night people began to be afraid. The game was still even; nobody had won. But the Sun was coming and coming, and the night animals had to run away. Bear jumped up in such a hurry that he put his right foot in his left moccasin, and his left foot in his right moccasin.

The Sun was full up now, and all the other night animals were gone. Bear went after them as fast as he could in his wrong moccasins, rocking and waddling from side to side, and shouting, "Wait for me! Wait for me!"

But nobody stopped or waited, and Bear had to go waddling along, just the way he has done ever since.

And because nobody won the game, the day and night took turns from that time on. Everybody had the same time to come out and live his life the way he wanted to as everybody else.

SOURCE: Alice Marriott and Carol K. Rachlin. "Why the Bear Waddles When He Walks." *American Indian Mythology.* New York: Crowell, 1968.

To get ready for war, Comanche men did a war dance and prayed for strength. They painted their faces and bodies with symbols of their power. Warriors wore headdresses with buffalo horns and carried their fancy shields.

Comanche warriors traveled long distances and attacked without warning. Male enemies were usually tortured and killed. Women and children, though, were often brought back to camp as captives.

Vision quest

A young Comanche man would go on a vision quest (a search for his spirit guide). First, he climbed to the top of a hill. He stopped four times on the way to smoke a pipe and pray. He stayed alone on the hill for four days and nights with no food or water. In the morning, he prayed to the sun for a vision. When he had his vision, the young man went home to ask the medicine man to explain it. The young man then knew what items he needed for his medicine bundle. The medicine bundle showed his personal power and his tie to the supernatural.

When it was time for his vision quest, a Comanche man stayed on a hill without food or water for four days and nights.

Courtship and marriage

A young man was allowed to marry after he had done his vision quest and been part of a war party. Most Comanche men did not marry until they had shown that they could provide for a wife and children, though.

The man sent his family to meet with the chosen woman's family to get their consent to the match. The woman had no say in the matter.

Comanche babies were wrapped in decorated carriers called cradleboards.

Once the arrangements had been made, the man proposed. To do this, he gave the woman's male relatives horses. There was no formal wedding. The couple just went to the man's tepee. The Comanche believed that no woman should stay single. So, a man sometimes married his wife's sister, too.

Children

Children were named by a prominent member of the tribe. If the child fell ill or seemed to have bad luck, the family might choose a new name.

Games and festivities

The Comanche hold a Homecoming Powwow each year in July. Powwows are celebrations that feature songs and dances. In 1972, a group of Comanche founded the Little Ponies. This group holds powwows and sponsors other events to help keep tribal customs alive.

A Comanche man performs a traditional dance at an Indian arts festival.

Current tribal issues

Some issues divide the Comanche tribe. For example, conflicts have come up between Christians and members of the Native American Church. There is also tension between full-blood and mixed-blood Comanche.

Chief Quanah Parker

Notable People

Quanah Parker (lived from about 1852 to 1911), a Comanche leader, was the son of Cynthia Parker, a white woman who had been kidnapped as a child. She came to prefer the Comanche way of life and married a powerful member of the tribe, Peta Nocona. Quanah Parker led the Comanche against U.S. troops until he had to surrender in 1875.

LaDonna Harris (1931–) is a Comanche woman who has fought to win equal opportunity for Indian people.

For more information

Hagan, William T. *Quanah Parker, Comanche Chief.* Norman: University of Oklahoma Press, 1993.

Rollings, Willard H. *The Comanche.* New York: Chelsea House, 1989.

Sultzman, Lee. *Comanche History.* http://www.dickshovel.com

Wallace, Ernest, and E. Adamson Hoebel. *The Comanches: Lords of the Southern Plains.* Norman: University of Oklahoma Press, 1952.

LaDonna Harris

Glossary

Comanchería land of the Comanche

Peyote a drug used in certain religious practices that may give the user visions

Raid an attack on land or a settlement, usually to steal food and other goods

Reservation land set aside and given to Native Americans

Ritual something that is a custom or done in a certain way

Tribe a group of people who live together in a community

Index